PUBLICADO POR ROBERT CORBIN

BODY LANGUAGE

@ Berry Cox

Publicado por Robert Corbin

@ Berry Cox

Body Language: The Ultimate Guide on

Natural Communication and Sharing

Expression with Others

ISBN 978-87-94477-97-0

TABLE OF CONTENTS

Chapter 1

Relating context to the nonverbal cues

How you or anyone interprets body language greatly depends on the surroundings, situations and the environment. Let's assume that you and one of your friend is talking to each other. And in this situation you see that he is crossing his arms and touching his face often. On the surface, you can readily understand that he is feeling uncomfortable. But you can't understand why he feels uncomfortable just by reading his body language. To know the "why" of the situation you need context.

Now you could ask what exactly this "context" is. Simply put, context is the essential elements that you need to look at to accurately read someone's mind. You need to consider three essential things to relate the context to the nonverbal cues.

Firstly, you need to consider the environment where your conversation is taking place. In order to decode your partner fully, you need to understand what things in the environment they are reacting to. For instance, a person could feel uncomfortable if they are in a crowded place. They could be annoyed by the noise. If suddenly someone's ex pops up, it's bound to make the person uncomfortable. So, observe the environment. Notice what the person reacts to and relate it to their body language to have a better guess of their emotional state.

The second thing that's equally important is the conversation itself. How a conversation goes can also point at various things. For instance, if you notice that after a particular opinion of yours, the other person's voice changes, it can mean that they don't find your opinion appealing.

Sometimes a question that you ask can also make them uncomfortable. So these are some important aspects that you need to consider before you can reach a conclusion.

Lastly, their recent experiences and feelings will also affect their body postures. You have to consider that they may have passed through a lot of events before finally meeting you and how they will behave with you will depend on those events. For instance, when someone has a bad day at work, they might come back home and still ponder of those stressful events which will make them give off negative nonverbal cues.

Chapter 2

Hidden Body Language Secrets

The knowledge of body language used nonverbally to communicate is used by law enforcement to detect nonverbal clues, cues, or flags of suspects and those who may inflict crimes on society. These skills acquired by law enforcement may also aid the victims of crime. By using the knowledge of clues, cues, or flags law enforcement in all areas of the country and overseas can better protect citizens from criminals and those wishing to do harm to their fellow man. Even the FBI (Federal Bureau of Investigations) uses the practice of body language to get information from potential criminals, convicted criminals, and those who break the law. Have you ever heard someone say, "You're using your poker face?"

If you've never played the game of Poker; members in a poker game study the faces of their fellow opponents to see if something in their face will give the hand they're holding away.

In the case of a man holding a full-house; 2-Aces and 3-Kings; if the man holding the full-house isn't very careful, he may grin and tip off the other players that he has a good hand. If he looks up and his eyes are sparkling with glee, those around the table may calculate he is holding a winning hand even though he may have given the others the impression he had nothing worth holding in his hand. So the man needs to show an expression on his face that is neither showing nor telling of the cards he holds in his hand IF he is to bluff the others into believing he is holding nothing of worth.

Personal Space in Nonverbal Body Language Communication

Nonverbal communication also involves the distance at which we stand from someone we're speaking with. The acceptable distance for most folks from the person they're speaking with is an arm's length. If you stick your arm out in front of you and do a circumference, you'll get an idea of your personal boundary around you. This will give you an idea of the acceptable personal space belonging to you.

Some people infringe on personal space by standing within your personal space. Have you encountered others who stand too close to you when they are speaking with you? How does it make you feel? Do you take two steps backward to lengthen the space between you only to have the other person take two steps forward toward you? Some individuals seem clueless as to what personal space means.

In business matters, salespersons may use this technique to make you feel you can trust them in your dealings with them. Be careful, however, because this can act as a double-edged sword. For some, it may appear you are trustworthy and capable. For others, it may signify mistrust and alienation, as you standing closer to them may make them feel uncomfortable. Best practice seems to be to keep the arm's length model when communicating with others.

Someone may think they are keeping a secret when you ask them a question that requires a response of, *yes.* The person says nothing, but unconsciously the person shakes their head up-and-down signifying, *yes.*

A shrug of the shoulders by a person being interrogated may indicate in a nonverbal matter that they *could care less about what you're saying.*

Being on the lookout for nonverbal signals in the form of clues, cues, or flags may provide much-needed information over and beyond spoken words, or any other verbal communication.

Chapter 3

Simple Techniques to Start with

Learning how to read people is an art form, and it involves tapping into sense that we might not usually use. Part of being a human is reading unspoken cues given to us by the people around us. This helps us not only to decipher how they feel and what they think, but what they are like on a deeper level than the surface. Most people who wish to learn how to interpret nonverbal and verbal signals have a hope to see to the core of other people instead of just the everyday masks most people put forth. Logic is not enough to help you figure out a person's entire story, or even all of what they feel at this very moment. You have to tap into other important sources of data and information so you can figure out how to read intuitive signals that everyone is constantly giving off.

Looking Past Biases to Analyze People

To read people, you need to know how to surrender your biases, preconceived ideas, ego clashes, resentments, and any baggage you have that could be clouding your judgment and preventing you from accurately reading someone. The ideal here is to stay objective and observe data without twisting it in your mind to fit your prejudices or biases. This is no easy task. Whether your hope is to read your partner, co-worker, or even your boss, in order to read people, you have to break down some walls within yourself. Although our intellectual minds are undeniably brilliant and advanced, they can limit us. Those who are good at reading others accurately have trained themselves to see what isn't obvious to the rest of us. They have accessed advanced senses in order to access valuable and intuitive information and insight.

Observing Physical, Nonverbal Clues

Studies have shown us that words only communicate a portion of what we are really saying, while other cues communicate the rest. In this area, although it may sound counterintuitive, the idea is to let go of thinking about trying to read nonverbal signals. Getting too analytical or intense about it will only hinder your progress. Remember to stay calm, comfortable, and just observe and perceive. As humans, we are like other animals in that we can instinctively read each other. Most of the time, it's a matter of getting out of our own way in order to make this happen.

Appearance does Matter: Appearance is something to pay attention to when it comes to trying to read people. As you attempt to observe them, notice if they are dressed up in nice, business-themed clothes that shout ambition or a t-shirt and jeans combo that appear to signal rest and relaxation. Are they wearing a necklace with a large religious symbol on it, or perhaps a revealing outfit? All of this can tell you what this person's motives are.

Pay Attention to Posture: When you are observing a person's posture, notice whether they appear confident with their head held up, or whether they appear to cower as they walk. Do they stick out their chest as a signal of dominance, or try to walk by unnoticed? A person's posture says a lot about them, even if it's only about their mood at that particular moment.

Physical Indicators and Movements: The direction a person leans in can be very telling; for instance, someone who leans toward you likes you, and someone who leans away from someone typically doesn't feel very favorably about them. Another common sign is the crossing of the legs or arms. When someone does this, it can signal that they are feeling defensive or angry. Keep in mind that this isn't a foolproof sign, and that someone might just be cold.

If someone appears to be trying to hide their hands, in their pockets for example, it may indicate that they are attempting to hide something or feel uncomfortable. On a similar note, someone who is biting their lips or picking at their nails, this could indicate anxiety, feeling pressured, or feeling awkward. In addition to this, someone pursing their lips could mean that they feel bitter or angry, while clenched teeth signal tension or frustration.

Learning to Intuitively read Body Language

It's possible to interpret a person's inner-state beyond what they are saying using your intuition, which relies on gut feelings and instinct rather than just logic. It's unspoken data that we receive through images, sudden moments of insight, and bodily perceptions, instead of analytic logical reasoning. If you hope to gain understanding of a person, what matters is who they are deep down, not superficial aspects of them. Tapping into your intuition can help you look beyond the obvious to get a fuller picture. Here are some intuitive clues to look out for when reading people:

Noticing Gut Feelings:

Pay attention to what your gut is telling you, particularly when you are very first meeting someone, which gives you a reaction based on pure instinct before your mind chimes in. This can show you whether you feel comfortable or not. These reactions happen instantly and tell you whether or not you can trust someone. These reactions evolved with us for a reason, so make sure you honor them and pay attention.

Spontaneous Insights:

 Pay special attention to sudden flashes of information or insight that come to you about someone. If you are like the average person, you have a constant stream of thoughts flowing through your mind, which makes it easy to lose important data that could be useful to you. Make it a point to notice these things.

Noticing Empathy:

If you are a particularly sensitive person, you should be able to feel other people's moods empathetically or intuitively. When you interact with someone who is very joyful, you feel it intensely as though it's your joy, and the same goes for negative emotions. This can be an accurate gauge for what another person is feeling, depending on your own personality.

Sensing the Emotions of Others

Emotions make up the impressions we give to other people, which are then registered in an intuitive way. Some people are easy and nice to spend time around, while others feel draining and make you want to run away. Reading and analyzing people has a lot to do with learning how to consciously sense this. Here are some key tips for doing just that:

Pay Attention to Eyes:

It's no secret that eyes are very expressive and revealing. Take some time to start observing the people around you and their eyes. Do they appear to be frustrated, interested, and intelligent? Do they appear to be uncomfortable or anxious? Another very useful part of the face to look at is the eyebrows. Are the person's eyebrows pointing upward or downward? This can tell a lot about the mood they are in and whether or not they are listening.

Pay Attention to Physical Touch:

 Another way to start accurately reading people is to pay attention to physical touch such as a hug or a handshake. Next time you encounter this with someone, notice whether it feels inviting and warm, or cold and calculating. Does the hug feel confident and comfortable, or nervous and stand-offish? These can tell you a lot about the person's inner-state.

Laugh and Voice:

The volume and tone of voice a person uses says a lot about what they are feeling. When a person talks a lot and has a boisterous laugh, it's safe to assume that they are quite confident. When a person who usually sounds this way sounds very different, it's an indication that they are feeling something else. For someone who is usually really quiet and withdrawn who is being louder, something is obviously up with them. These are all the types of clues you need to be watching for in order to learn how to read body language effectively and accurately.

All of this information is useful for reading people, along with other indicators such as how well you know them, whether or not they are comfortable with you, and the context and situation you find yourself in. Someone who is very happy and boisterous at a concert, obviously, is not always naturally that way, and it's likely just the situation making them feel that way. Someone who appears sad at a party might be a naturally sullen person or they might just be having a bad day. Take all of this into consideration before you jump to conclusions about people and their body language. Over time, you will get better at reading it accurately.

Chapter 4

Daily Gestures

Ever wonder why "welcoming with open arms" is understood as receiving or accepting eagerly? That's because having open arms is usually associated with hospitality and approachableness. Open hands or palms, on the other hand, may mean submissiveness or that the person's defenses are down, or more positively, it may mean honesty.

Chapter 3 mainly talks about the different gestures we see every day, including our shoulders, arms, and hand gestures. While our faces communicate our feelings and emotions, our arms communicate our level of confidence and dominance.

SHOULDERS

Raising the shoulders is often used to convey when the person doesn't know or understand the subject of the conversation, and is more commonly called a shrug. But shoulders say much more than that you do not know.

In fact, think of a person with a well-defined, broad shoulder... what does it tell you? Shoulders are a symbol for hierarchy, which is why we perceive people with broad shoulders as the authority, thus assuming they know more. However, the most prominent functional and nonverbal feature of the shoulders is that they tell you what the person is feeling through posture. Remember when your mom and dad just magically asked you 'what's making you feel down?' Or when a friend asked you whether you were okay? You never told anyone, they just knew. Well, here's the news, your shoulders gave you away. A person's posture can definitely communicate his or her emotions.

Good posture communicates confidence and certainty. When a person sits or stands straight, they acquire respect from others. An impression of esteem hangs around him or her. It is also an indication of a joyful and confident mood.

When a person is slouching down, sadness and insecurity are expressed. The spine is hunched, and the head is hung low. This posture indicates that the person is feeling unhappy. The person may not explicitly tell others what they truly feel, but their hunched posture is an indicator that he or she is feeling down.

Apart from those mentioned above, the shoulders can also reveal whether a person is lying or not. Lack of confidence may be expressed through hunched shoulders; this can mean that the person is unsure of himself and might be hiding something. The same could be interpreted if there is a sudden rise of the shoulders. For example, if you ask a colleague whether he could get a task done by the deadline, and he answers

with a slight rise of the shoulders, then he is

maybe unsure. It would be helpful if you try to

prod for more answers. This way you could help

or try to remedy the uncertainty.

HANDS

Imagine yourself offering a high five to your

friend. To which direction is your palm facing? Is it

facing upwards or downwards?

Palms, though often overlooked, are very helpful

in determining the level of authority of the

person. Notice the people around you, and try to

determine whether this co-worker is dominant, or

if a friend is submissive.

When your palm is gestured open and facing

upwards, you are more likely to be the receiving

type. This gesture is often interpreted as non-

threatening and submissive. In work places, when

orders are given with open palms, they are less

likely to be interpreted as domineering which makes the probability of the person to perform the orders higher. They are seen as more of a request than a command. On the other hand, people who give orders with their palms facing downwards may be seen as antagonistic, especially if the person is your co-worker and you both have the same work status! You are less likely to follow the request. So, if you ever want to ask for a request from somebody, you face your palm to that one direction accordingly. Aside from knowing a person's authority, palms are also a good way of determining if a person is lying. Open palms usually indicate that the person is telling the truth. If you ask a person questions, they will expose their palms to you to tell you they are telling the truth.

During meeting presentations, observe that when presenters conceal their hands they're either trying to hide something or lying. This is the reason why, when people are trying to sell something, they intentionally display their hands to show you that they are telling the truth. This is also the reason people raise their palms to indicate that they're innocent, like during an arrest. And in court trials, placing the palms on a Bible signifies that you will be telling the truth. Another one of the most common gestures that we use daily, especially in the office, is the handshake, as already discussed in the previous chapter. A handshake can establish a relationship. Aside from handshakes, smiles, postures, and high fives, there are other gestures that are used daily, especially in corporate settings.

Nodding

During a discussion, a nod is interpreted as a nonverbal agreement. A nod, simply put, signifies a "Yes." Most cultures use nodding to confirm an idea, but there are cultures in which they shake their heads instead, like in India. However, nodding seems to be innate to human nature since people who are blind still know how to nod to agree. A nod is a very strong tool for persuasion. When you nod from time to time when a person is speaking, you are more likely to motivate that person to talk more. Of course, this would depend on the pace of your nodding. Slow, regular nods can mean agreement, while deliberate, fast nods can mean impatience. Affirmative feelings can be achieved by nodding, and, likewise, affirmative feelings lead to nodding. And since gestures can be easily mirrored, if you nod while you speak, people are more likely to nod with you. In this way, you have already unconsciously persuaded them.

If you are on the listening side, try accompanying your nod with a 'Considering' or 'Evaluating' stance. Place your thumb and forefinger under your chin, and discreetly move your fingers from side to side. It would also be more effective if you look intently at the speaker.

Shake

Shaking your head from side to side is the counterpart of nodding. People shake their heads when there is something with which they do not agree. When a person shakes their head, they may have an aversion toward your ideas or comments. You could try convincing the person by trying another approach.

A head-shake could also be a way for a person to say that he or she did not quite get what was said. A more emotional head-shake would be when a person is in grief or shock. The shaking would be more rhythmic as empathy is shown. Disbelief could also make a person shake their head, especially when there is dissonance.

Shrug

A nod is a 'Yes,' a shake is a 'No,' and the shrug is the one nearest to a 'Maybe.' As discussed before, a shrug is given when a person doesn't know or understand. The head is pulled down, and the shoulders drawn up to indicate an unsure response. Another form of shrug is the head shrug. This gesture is often displayed in the presence of a superior. The tendency to present the self as smaller is implied during the head shrug. It also connotes a submissive and obedient attitude.

Hands-on-hips

Hands-on-hips is the stance of getting ready for action. This gesture makes the person look larger than he they already are. The hands are placed on the hips with elbows pointed out and upwards. The elbows look like weapons that the person could use for battle. You see athletes doing this while waiting for the competition to start. This nonverbal cue is telling us that they are getting ready. You could also observe this at work. Notice people who are in this stance; they're probably getting ready for a presentation, an argument, and the like. In a moment, that person is going to be assertive and/or aggressive.

The Legs-Spread

This nonverbal cue is usually seen in men. This means that they are trying to establish themselves as dominant and authoritative. Women around men who display this gesture would feel intimidated and defensive, and will respond by legs-crossing. Just like any dominating stance, this can be countered by explicitly pointing it out, especially if it's making you or anyone feel uncomfortable.

Lint-Picking

This is a more elusive gesture, as only a few can detect what this means. A person picks out imaginary lint, or dusts, or loose threads on his clothes when he or she is trying to object on something but somehow cannot get it out. You can get their opinion, though, by asking them directly.

Head Up

This position signals dominance and superiority. They execute the head up to gain more imaginary height and to 'look down' on people. This gesture is usually used by people who want to impose and highlight their superiority.

Head Down

Head down indicates that the person is in a judging position. The person is critically assessing the situation; a negative appraisal will probably follow. An aggressive attitude may succeed the head down position. Once the situation is remedied, the person's head might return to natural position.

The Catapult

Just like the legs-spread, this gesture is more often utilized my men. This is done seated, with the hands at the back of the head, and with the elbows pointed out. This position is used to intimidate others and to display authority and expertise. The person in this position is likely telling you that he knows everything. Professionals such as businessmen, lawyers, and accountants are seen in this position. Managers are also seen in this position in the presence of their subordinates, but not with their superiors. Women can counter this position by remaining in a standing position. He may decide to take a break from doing this position to continue the conversation.

The Cowboy Stance

This stance is another indicator of dominance and territoriality. In this position, men, typically, seemingly display their genital area by framing it with their hands while the thumbs are tucked into their pockets. It is called such because in TV shows, cowboys are projected in this way. The Cowboy Stance may also signal sexual aggression. Women who try to execute this position are seen as sexually assertive.

These gestures we see every day can be used to unlock different hidden and unconscious relations with other people. Appropriate actions and responses can be done once you understand and know how to interpret body language. It can also be used to enhance good communication in a team or a group of friends, and eliminate possible misunderstandings that may arise. Counter-gestures can be done, especially for movements that are used to intimidate. Aside from the different gestures we witness every day, we also have the emotions and feelings of people. Emotions can be communicated with the face. However, some people are expert at hiding their feelings. Con artists are the best players in this field. You can rarely see them flash a deceptive expression, which is why they are almost never caught. But a technique has already been developed by a team of psychologists led by Dr. Paul Ekman, as will be discussed in the next chapter. Using the person's unconscious, fleeting expressions, one can see what the person actually feels.

Chapter 5

The Four Main Types of Body Language

The way you act and the way your body moves
can provide clues about who you really are.
Without the use of words, we communicate nonverbally via our body language, whether we are
aware of it or not.

The way you move, sit, stand, and walk may be
able to help you understand who you really are.
Each one of us expresses our body language in
one of four ways:

- precise and bold movement

- dynamic and determined movement light and
  bouncy movement

- soft and fluid movement

.

Each of these movements has its own meanings and may coincide with one of the four types of energy. Energy profiling is a profiling system that is based on movement. Everything in your natural world has a corresponding dominant energy type. The two most powerful assessment tools used to discover your energy type are your body language and your facial features.

To help you further understand, this chapter teaches you what the four types of body language are.

Upward, light animated

You "sashay" with a buoyant and bouncy spring in your steps. You sit and stand with many different movements, and you shift your position quite often. You may come off as restless to others because you don't like being confined to an office desk and sitting and standing still for long periods.

You are often seen sitting with your legs crisscrossed, or comfortably flat on the floor.

Fluid, flowing, soft

You have a graceful walk that is soft and classy. You are likely to take longer steps while keeping your feet close to the ground. There is an obvious absence of bouncing while walking, instead, your movements are fluid and flowing naturally. You sit and you stand in the shape of an S curve or you are relaxed holding your head on the side.

Active, reactive, substantial

You walk confidently and full of determination. Your steps are quick and brisk. People can hear you coming. They can even hear you sit because your movements are quite deliberate. You create different angles when you sit and stand. Your legs are often crossed, with one leg pulled up under you. Your head is usually cocked to the side, while your hands are on your waist. You may also have your body bent at the waist.

Bold, constant, still

Your walk is stately and upright. Your limbs and body have little movements while you walk. You sit upright too, with a straight posture, with your feet firmly on the ground and your hands are either folded or hanging to your sides. You project a proper and formal look when you sit and stand. Runway models are the dominant Type 4 Energy. They are naturally poised, erect, upright, and structured in their movements. They maintain a perfect posture, with their back and shoulders straight up.

Chapter 6

The Need to Understand Body Language

Understanding body language is often the first step to beginning and maintaining great friendships

Well, you may not care to make friends, which is fine really if that's your thing. But if you are keen on making friends or even just improving your existing friendships, then you need to understand body language to communicate effectively and understand what others are trying to communicate.

Let's assume that a good number of people who meet you either withdraw or project some hostility toward you. You may be good-looking and even smell nice on the daily trip to work. But still, the people you meet almost always grow cold, and most of your relationships never seem to progress from the first encounter.

The usual assumption for most of us is that there is something inherently noxious about us, or that most of the people we meet are shallow or perhaps uninterested in us. But oftentimes, the truth is that your body language has a cold edge to it and more so, your body language assessment skills are terrible, so that your responses seem insensitive or detached.

Once you understand body language, you can fix such problems very quickly. It becomes easier to make new friends. Maintaining friendships ceases to become an overly difficult task. As some might put it, you eventually become a 'natural.'

Understanding body language positively impacts your dating skills

Once you build body language comprehension, it becomes easy to tell if somebody is interested in you. Quite a number of people miss out on dating and even marrying great people because they were unable to read body language that indicated the other person was interested.

Understanding body language helps in maintaining and growing your marriage

A marriage where one or both parties has poor comprehension of body language is usually doomed, and a major reason why divorce rates in the US stand over 50% is because the current generation is far too obsessed with technology and 'fast' stuff to properly learn old-fashioned stuff like body language and how to interact with people.

For example, when your wife says, with a slightly raised voice, "Josh, or Honey?" then it could be her way of saying "I'm getting ready to ask a favor of you" or "We need to talk for a bit." If your body language skills are proper, you will adjust mentally to the situation and the ensuing interaction will flow smoother. The same is not the case for those who have no clue about body language.

Positive body language skills are a massive help with regard to increasing your confidence

As you become smarter at reading other people's body language and catching cues, you will ultimately feel less and less anxious about what you can expect in social situations. You will almost always know what to expect before it happens to you. This preparedness and ability to predict interactions will breed confidence in a way few things do. You will be in control and you will know it.

I hope you now know why it is critical to learn and understand body language. Let us now move on to some surprising facts about body language.

Chapter 7

The Cues that Tell It All: Context Trumps Words

Universally, there are certain facial expressions that demolish all cultural divides. Researchers conclude that each one over the planet, happiness, sadness, surprise, fear, disgust, and anger are all expressed within the same manner. Gesturing, also as touching, gives off certain signals that assist with emotions.

However, nonverbal communication essentially means reading between the lines and seeking truth within the midst of words. An individual could also be saying one thing, but their tone means another. Researchers have grouped nonverbal communication into five categories. Let's consider them each.

Repetition

When engaging during a conversation, it's useful to repeat what the opposite person has said so on improve memory. When an individual verbally repeats what you said to them, they're demonstrating that your statement matters. They need to be ready to access that information at a later time. Additionally, this might be used as a sign that they're taking note of what you're saying. Take care, though, as an excessive amount of repetition might be an irritation to some. They'll misunderstand your listening cues as condescending as this is often what mothers do to children once they learn to talk.

Contradiction

Contradiction is one among the more obvious cues that signal disapproval. Often times, these subtle contradictions might be wont to demean another or express dominance. One among the first samples of this happens within the workplace. For instance, a controlling manager overhears her employee speaking with a customer. The customer is asking a few specific protocol. The worker is attempting to explain a neater thanks to accomplish her goal. Upon hearing, the manager immediately steps in, tells the worker that her way is wrong and proceeds to direct the customer herself. Imagine how that employee feels. Not only was she embarrassed ahead of a client, but her notability was questioned. This contradiction caused the customer to look at the worker as someone who isn't well-versed. The manager could have handled things during a more graceful manner, and certain, this was done out of an effort to prove dominance.

Substitutions

Do you remember that look your mother gave you when she meant what she said? Likely, you'll envision those stern eyes, scrunched mouth, and high demeanor. Your mother didn't need to utter one phrase for you to know that your current behavior was unacceptable. Daily, we use substitutions as a way to speak. These intense glares or slight glances can speak volumes to people that know one another well. They'll also indicate emphasis on a particular command. Dogs operate primarily through vocal substitutions. Once you loom over a dog while stating, "Back," they know that area is off limits to them. The particular word is being substituted for a clear action.

Complimenting

When a young man performs well at his baseball, onlookers can see the coach patting him on the rear or maybe giving him a high five. These outward displays of approval are well-known cues that signify employment well done. We may provides a wink, hand gesture, or maybe a hug to precise proud emotions towards others. This mild stamp of approval crosses masculine and female roles also. Football players are often seen patting the butts of their teammates to suggest employment well done. When conducted between romantic interests, this might be an outward sexual invitation.

Accenting

This occurs when people want their voices to be heard. They'll slam their bedroom doors after yelling a remark, or clap their hands to precise seriousness. This will be likened to accenting a selected word. That tiny dash brings emphasis to at least one or more of the noted letters. Thus, it alerts the reader to vary their pronunciation. Similarly, accenting in nonverbal cues could signal a change of behavior. When analyzing individuals with deep-rooted insecurities, they'll rely heavily on accenting their words so as to seem dominant.

They're hoping to ignite fear in their subjects as a way of control.

Gestures can accentuate a conversation and make excitement. Typically, individuals who utilize gestures are described as, "people who talk with their hands." These movements can emphasize the plot of a story or maybe bring light to a discourse. They're descriptive in nature, and are wont to keeping the eye of an audience or a private. Speechmaking classes place an excellent deal of weight on the importance of using gestures in their delivery. They carry warmth to the words being spoken additionally to liveliness. One of the first ways to create a person's connection is thru touch. The embracing touch coming from a lover or a stranger can alleviate stress and make a way of community. When grieving, oftentimes, words from well-intended individuals aren't enough. However, a chump of the hand speaks, "I am here for you," during a way that words could never express. The rationale being is that touching is an action. You're physically showing someone your interest in them. Additionally, touching hands can signify a person's personality. Certain managers judge potential candidates based upon their handshake. If they encounter a weak shake, the boss can devour on their timid nature. They'll recoil from hiring them during a fast-paced environment. On the opposite hand, a firm shake exudes confidence. The hiring manager may consider that candidate because they didn't display fear. Across various cultures, the quantity of private space given is varied. East Asian cultures typically stand about one to 2 inches faraway from the person they're engaging with. This displays a symbol of respect and interest. Within the us, however, we may view that spatial closeness as intruding. We may even feel uncomfortable on what the person's intentions are. However, creating an excessive amount of space could trigger your householder into thinking you don't want to be around them. Creating a balanced view of spatial awareness is vital to communicating effectively. Take a glance at the space between the tip of your pointer finger and your inner elbow. This is often the right amount of allotted space which will allow you to converse comfortably together with your partner.

The manner during which someone speaks also can indicate personality traits. Usually, grammar school teachers will speak to their students during a high-pitched voice, because it ignites excitement and is inviting. However, that level of pleasure might not be warranted at an all-adult function. In fact, if they tried to talk to a different adult therein manner, the receiving adult may take it because the person being condescending. It's useful to think about the tone during which you're speaking so as to not come off as being rude, sarcastic, or maybe flirty. Creating a balanced manner of speaking while interjecting inflections when necessary will assist you to effectively communicate without offense. Nonverbal communication are often acquired through analyzing simple cues that occur daily. You'll ask yourself, "When someone speaks to me during this way, how do I feel?" Or, "Am I comfortable when somebody else is that this on the brink of me?" By asking yourself these simple questions, you'll be ready to effectively communicate with others while learning on their cues.

Chapter 8

How to analyze people?

The ability to read others will greatly affect how you deal with them. When you understand how another person is feeling, you can adapt your message and communication style to make sure it is received in the best way possible. But what should you be listening for? And what other signs can tip you off to what someone is thinking or feeling? Whether you're reading your boss, co-worker, or partner to understand people accurately you must surrender biases, some walls must come down. As brilliant as the intellect is, you have to be willing to let go of old, limiting ideas. People who read others well are trained to read the invisible. They have learned to utilize super-senses to look further than where you usually put your attention to access life-changing intuitive insights. Research has shown that words account for only 7 percent of how we communicate whereas our body language 55% and voice tone 30% represent the rest. Here, the surrender to focus on is letting go of trying too hard to read body language cues. Don't get overly intense or analytical. Stay relaxed and fluid. Be comfortable, sit back, and simply observe.

Pay Attention to Appearance

When reading others notice: Are they wearing a power suit and well-shined shoes, dressed for success, indicating ambition? Jeans and t-shirt indicating comfort with being casual? A tight top with cleavage is a seductive choice?

Notice Posture

When reading people's posture, ask yourself: Do they hold their head high, confident? Or do they walk indecisively or cower, a sign of low self-esteem? Do they swagger with a puffed-out chest, a sign of a big ego?

Watch for Physical Movements

Leaning and distance. Observe where people lean. Generally, we lean toward those we like and away from those we don't. Crossed arms and legs is a pose that suggests defensiveness, anger, or self-protection. When people cross their legs they tend to point the toes of the top leg towards the person they are most at ease with.

Hiding one of the hands - When people place their hands in their laps, pockets, or put them behind their back it suggests that they are hiding something.

Lip biting or cuticle picking - When people bite or lick their lips or pick their cuticles they are trying to soothe themselves under pressure or in an awkward situation.

Interpret Facial Expression

Emotions can become etched on our faces. Deep frown lines suggest worry or over-thinking. Crow's feet are the smile lines of joy. Pursed lips signal anger, contempt, or bitterness. A clenched jaw and teeth grinding are signs of tension. Emotions are a stunning expression of our energy, the "vibe" we give off. We register these with intuition. Some people feel good to be around; they improve your mood and vitality. Others are draining; you instinctively want to get away. This "subtle energy" can be felt inches or feet from the body, though it's invisible. In Chinese medicine, it's called chi, a vitality that's essential to health.

Sense People's Presence

This is the overall energy we emit, not necessarily congruent with words or behavior. It's the emotional atmosphere surrounding us like a rain cloud or the sun. As you read people notice: Do they have a friendly presence that attracts you? Or are you getting the willies, making you back off?

Watch People's Eyes

Our eyes transmit powerful energy. Just as the brain has an electromagnetic signal extending beyond the body, studies indicate that the eyes project this too. Take time to observe people's eyes. Are they caring? Are they sexy? Are they mean? Are they angry? Also determine: Is there someone at home in their eyes, indicating a capacity for intimacy? Or do they seem to be guarded or hiding?

3. Notice the Feel of a Handshake, Hug, and Touch

We share emotional energy through physical contact much like an electrical current. Ask yourself, does a handshake or hug feel warm, comfortable or confident? Or is it off-putting so you want to withdraw? Are people's hands clammy, signaling anxiety? Or limp suggesting being non-committal and timid?

4. Listen for Tone of Voice and Laugh

The tone and volume of our voice can tell much about our emotions. Sound frequencies create vibrations. When reading people, notice how their tone of voice affects you. Ask yourself: Does their tone feel soothing? Or is it abrasive, snippy, or whiny?

Decoding the mouth

If someone's smiling, that's a good sign, right? Not necessarily. Different smiles mean different things. The same goes for the position of someone's lips.

Smiles

With a true, genuine smile, the corners of the mouth turn up and the eyes narrow and wrinkle at the corners.

Insincere smiles generally don't involve the eyes.

They can happen in response to discomfort.

A smirk or partial smile that follows a

microexpression of displeasure or contempt can

suggest uncertainty, disdain, or dislike.

A smile accompanied by lasting eye contact, a

long glance, or a head tilt can suggest attraction.

Lips

Compressed or narrowed lips can suggest unease.

Quivering lips can suggest fear or sadness.

Pursed lips may indicate anger or disagreement.

Open, slightly parted lips tend to mean someone

feels relaxed or generally at ease.

Decoding of eyes

Eyes can convey a lot of information about

someone's mood and level of interest.

1. Blinking

People tend to blink rapidly when under some

sort of stress. You may have heard that rapid

blinking often suggests dishonesty, but this isn't always the case.

Someone's blinking may speed up when they're:

working through a difficult problem

feeling uncomfortable

afraid or worried about something

Pupil dilation

Your pupils will typically dilate when you feel positively toward something or someone. These feelings might involve romantic attraction, but this isn't always the case. Dilation happens in response to the arousal of your nervous system, so you may also notice dilated pupils when someone's angry or afraid. When you don't like something, your pupils will usually contract, or get smaller.

3. Gaze direction

Your eyes tend to follow what you're interested in, so tracking the movement of someone's gaze can give you information about their mood.

If you're talking to someone whose eyes keep wandering toward the buffet table, they might have more interest in eating than talking at the moment. Someone looking toward the exit may want to leave. People also tend to move their eyes down or to one side when:
working through a problem
recalling information or memories
thinking about something difficult

Eye blocking

Blocking includes things like:
covering your eyes with a hand
closing your eyes briefly, such as in a long blink
rubbing your eyes
squinting

Blocking is generally unconscious, but it tends to suggest how you really feel. People often block their eyes when irritated, distressed, or faced with something they don't particularly want to do. It can also suggest disagreement or reluctance. You know the house needs a good cleaning, but when your partner suggests taking a day for chores, your hand might go to your eyes before you realize it.

5. Watching the arms and legs

Although people usually use their arms and legs to make purposeful gestures, movements that happen more instinctively can also reveal a lot about emotions.

Arms

People often cross their arms when feeling:

vulnerable

anxious

uninterested in considering another perspective

Interestingly, crossed arms can also suggest confidence. If someone crosses their arms while smiling, leaning back, or showing other signs of being at ease, they probably feel somewhat in control of the situation, rather than vulnerable. The arms can also give someone a sense of protection. Keep an eye out for behaviors like:

holding something against the chest

bringing an arm to rest on a chair or table

putting an arm out to create distance

using one arm to hold the other behind the back

These gestures subconsciously suggest that a person doesn't feel entirely comfortable with the situation and needs to steady or protect themselves in some way.

Legs and feet

The feet and legs can show nervousness and restlessness through:

tapping feet

leg jiggling

shifting from foot to foot

Crossed legs can also suggest an unwillingness to hear what someone has to say, especially when arms are also crossed. Feet can also reveal information. Note the direction a person's feet face during a conversation. If their feet point away, they may feel more like leaving the conversation than continuing it. If their feet point toward you, the person is likely enjoying the conversation and hoping to continue it.

Hands

Many people use gestures for emphasis when speaking. This can have some direct benefits, as researchTrusted Source suggests we tend to answer someone's question faster if they make gestures while asking. The more enthusiastic the gesture, the more excitement someone's likely feeling. It's also fairly common for people to gesture toward someone they feel particularly close to, often without realizing it.

Here are some more specific things to watch for:
Outstretched hands with palms up may be an unconscious reflection of openness.
Clenched fists can suggest anger or frustration, especially in someone trying to suppress these emotions. You might notice their facial expression remains neutral, even relaxed.
Instinctively touching the cheek might signal that someone is considering something carefully or has a lot of interest in what you're saying.
Breathing clues
Your breathing tends to pick up when you're under stress. This stress can be positive or negative, so someone breathing quickly may be:
excited

anxious

nervous or worried

A long, deep breath can suggest:

relief

anger

fatigue

Slower breaths typically suggest a state of calm or thoughtfulness. Ordinary breathing patterns may not stand out so much, but someone's breathing can seem very controlled or precise. This intentional control often happens when trying to suppress a strong emotion, such as anger.

Considering body positions

How someone stands or sits and where they do it can give you some clues about how they're feeling.

Chapter 9

Tips for Improving Your Nonverbal Communication

Solid communication abilities can help you in both your own and expert life. While verbal and composed communication abilities are significant, investigate has shown that nonverbal practices make up an enormous level of our everyday relational communication.

How might you improve your nonverbal communication abilities? The accompanying tips can assist you with figuring out how to read the nonverbal signals of others and upgrade your own capacity to impart viably.

Focus on Nonverbal Signals

Individuals can convey data from numerous points of view, so focus on things like eye contact, gestures, posture, body developments, and manner of speaking. These signals can pass on significant data that isn't articulated.

By giving nearer consideration to others' implicit practices, you will improve your own capacity to convey nonverbally.

Search for Incongruent Behaviors

In the event that somebody's words don't coordinate their nonverbal practices, you should give cautious consideration. For instance, somebody may disclose to you they are happy while scowling and gazing at the ground. Research has indicated that when words neglect to coordinate with nonverbal signals, individuals will in general disregard what has been said and center rather around implicit expressions of states of mind, considerations, and feelings. So when somebody says a certain something, however their body language appears to recommend something different, it tends to be valuable to give additional consideration to those unpretentious nonverbal signals.

Use Good Eye Contact

Great eye contact is another fundamental nonverbal communication ability. At the point when individuals neglect to look at others without flinching, it can appear as though they are dodging or attempting to conceal something. Then again, an excessive amount of eye contact can appear to be fierce or threatening.

While eye contact is a significant piece of communication, recall that great eye contact doesn't mean gazing steadily at someone. How might you tell what amount of eye contact is right?

Some communication specialists suggest interims of eye contact enduring four to five seconds. Powerful eye contact should feel normal and agreeable for both you and the individual you are talking with.

Pose Inquiries About Nonverbal Signals

On the other hand that you are confounded about someone else's nonverbal signals, don't be reluctant to pose inquiries. A smart thought is to rehash back your translation of what has been said and request explanation. A case of this may be, "So what you are stating is that..."
Once in a while just posing such inquiries can loan a lot of clearness to a circumstance. For instance, an individual may be radiating sure nonverbal signals since he has something different on his mind. By inquisitive further into his message and plan, you may show signs of improvement thought of what he is truly attempting to state.

Use Signals to Make Communication More Meaningful

Recollect that verbal and nonverbal communication cooperate to pass on a message. You can improve your expressed communication by utilizing body language that strengthens and bolsters what you are stating. This can be particularly valuable when making introductions or when addressing an enormous gathering of individuals.

For instance, if you will probably seem sure and arranged during an introduction, you will need to concentrate on imparting nonverbal signs that guarantee that others consider you to be confident and competent. Standing solidly in one spot, shoulder back, and your weight adjusted on the two feet is an extraordinary method to pause dramatically.

Take a gander at Signals as a Whole

Another significant piece of good nonverbal communication abilities includes having the option to adopt an increasingly all-encompassing strategy to what an individual is conveying.

A solitary motion can mean any number of things, or possibly nothing by any means.

The way to precisely reading nonverbal conduct is to search for gatherings of signals that fortify a typical point.

In the event that you place an excessive amount of accentuation on only one signal out of many, you may arrive at an off base decision about what an individual is attempting to state.

Think about the Context

At the point when you are speaking with others, generally consider the circumstance and the setting wherein the communication happens. A few circumstances require increasingly formal practices that may be deciphered contrastingly in some other setting.

Consider whether nonverbal practices are fitting for the specific circumstance. On the other hand that you are attempting to improve your own nonverbal communication, focus on approaches to make your signals coordinate the degree of convention required by the circumstance.

For instance, the body language and nonverbal communication you use at work are most likely totally different from the kind of signals you would send on an easygoing Friday night out with companions. Endeavor to coordinate your nonverbal signals to the circumstance to guarantee that you are passing on the message you truly need to send.

Be Aware That Signals Can be Misread

As per somewhere in the range of, a confident handshake shows a solid character while a feeble handshake is taken as an absence of backbone.

This model outlines a significant point about the plausibility of misreading nonverbal signals. A limp handshake may really show something different completely, for example, joint inflammation.

Continuously make sure to search for gatherings of conduct. An individual's general disposition is unmistakably more telling than a solitary signal saw in disengagement.

Chapter 10

The Six Absolute Truths of Body Language

To Tell the Truth broke the seal on body language, albeit from the tone inflection of voices hidden behind a studio panel. Recent television shows such as *Lie to Me* explored body language in much more detail and savvy viewers of other television shows learn how to notice non-verbal cues that reveal fascinating facts about the people making the hand gestures and facial expressions. Body language has become so in vogue that political commentators mention candidate non-verbal cues during in depth discussions of debates and public speeches.

However, not one television show or political pundit understands the six absolute truths of body language.

The So Called Experts Are Often Wrong about Body Language

Despite claims to the contrary, most so-called body language experts misread non-verbal cues. The biggest mistake surrounds hand gestures and the specific meaning hand gestures represent. A growing number of body language experts, although still in the minority, claim gestures of any kind can be ambiguous at best and deceitful at worst, if practiced by an accomplished con artist. Look at the universally understood meaning of someone crossing his or her arms. This gesture supposedly means the person has gone on the defensive, without uttering words. Yet, the person crossing his or her arms might simply be cold and crossing the arms brings comfort.

The bottom line: Gestures, especially gestures made with the hands, can mislead you into reading the wrong message sent by body language.

Don't Start with the Face

The face should be the culmination of reading body language, not the start of body language interpretation. By the time we reach adulthood, most of us have mastered the art of concealing our true feelings. Since getting along with friends, co-workers, and family members matters, we tend to learn how to mask our emotions. We pretend to listen, we pretend to laugh, and we pretend to empathize by controlling our facial expressions. Only under intense scrutiny do most adults reveal their true feelings, and hence the truth, via facial expressions. Think of a crime suspect put through a multi-hour interrogation. The bottom line: Save the face for last. The passage of time typically reveals thoughts and emotions by reading facial expressions.

The Face Does Reveal the Most Accurate Reading of Body Language

Have you ever interacted with someone that immediately unloads a boatload of emotion? Well, wait a few minutes for the tears to dry, before you make a reading of the person's body language. Most body language research concludes that the face provides the best way to read body language. Someone that tries to remain stoic might appear to succeed, but look for what behavioral scientists call micro expressions. These sudden flashes of facial changes indicate something else is boiling under the surface. Facial expressions frequently reveal someone's emotions and thought process.

The bottom line: Facial expressions provide the confirmation of what other types of body language express.

Intent, Not Meaning

Brain research demonstrates that our bodies feel the first wave of emotions, before transmitting the feelings to our conscious minds. For example, a rush of adrenaline through the body might eventually signal to the brain the feelings of anger, impatience, or happiness. Therefore, learning how to read body language requires you to focus on someone's intent, rather than the meaning of the body language. Since most adults successfully conceal emotions via hand gestures and facial expressions, we have to turn to the body to discern what exactly someone feels. Adults typically have a difficult time disguising feelings throughout the body.

The Bottom line: Focus on the body and discover intent.

Let Your Instincts Rule

We possess mirror brain neurons that ignite, whenever our conscious mind goes on alert to assimilate an emotion conveyed by another person. This means we shouldn't think about reading body language, but instead, allow our instincts to take over for accurately recognizing non-verbal cues. The expertise to read body language accurately has evolved in humans over centuries. Although still evolving, the expertise to read body language involves transferring knowledge stored in the unconscious region of the brain for use in the conscious mind.

The bottom line: Reading body language comes naturally; don't force it.

Read the Body Language of People You Know

People watching involves not only looking at people pass by, but also trying to discover what makes people tick or what people feel. This is an exercise in futility. If you want to learn what makes people tick, study the body language of people you know. Friends, family members, and professional associates offer non-verbal clues that you quickly pick up because of familiarity. In fact, you are much more proficient reading the body language of people you know than body language experts that have never met your friends, family members, or professional associates.

The bottom line: Save your body language expertise for people you know.

The unconscious part of the brain processes information in nanoseconds, before sending it to the conscious mind for you to take mental action. Reading body language uses both parts of the brain. However, a mostly ignored third brain resides near your beltline. Yes, the stomach possesses more neurons than the neurons possessed by the brain. Moreover, the gut connects directly to the unconscious part of the brain, making the organ the epicenter for the body language reading process. The stomach is especially effective for reading body language from someone that creates angst or poses a threat to your safety.

CHAPTER 11

UNDERSTANDING PEOPLE'S OUTWARD PERSONALITY

To understand the outward personality of people, this chapter will be particular about four facets that will help you in understanding people's lifestyle and personality.

At that moment when you meet a new person, the simple truth is that there are lots of things you don't know about them. All you have to go on at that moment are the outward clues you can pick out; their choice of clothing, physical appearance, speech pattern, and gait, for instance. In addition, you can also try to know more about people by watching the kind of people they mix with, their interactions with them, their social life and tastes. All these combine to form a mental image of the person's character profile within your mind.

In evaluating people, it is of utmost importance to be objective so that you do not just jump into preconceived conclusions. Most times, one sign is not enough to ascribe a particular character trait permanently to an individual. You need an aggregate of complementing attributes to reach such definitive conclusions. In fact, it is not advisable to reach a conclusion based on just observable traits and remain unyielding to contrary signs later on. Your conclusions are there to guide you even if they are correct a vast majority of the time. Outward attributes you see does not precisely indicate the personal qualities of those around you.

What you see

However, from their outward appearance, some important indicators that tell much about a person's personality are revealed. Part of these indicators includes the cloth they wear, hairstyle, perfume, and some other grooming habits that can be very useful in gaining the right perspective about a particular person. The thing is that many people make use of their style for their outward expression. Although there are some instances in which people dress in a particular way to change their look and probably make some impression that may not correlate to what they are going through internally

A person that has taken the time to look good, presentable, and neat has demonstrated attention to personal appearance to a reasonable extent. On the other hand, people that have an unkempt appearance, display ill social grace. Does that mean we can judge a person by the kind of clothes they put on alone? No! You need to consider the other variables before you make an erroneous blanket judgment. The only thing is that you can use that to form an initial opinion pending confirmative signs.

What you hear

The way people speak can betray their emotions and show the sort of people they are. People who speak using a steady intonation and a constant, smooth flow of words are typically identified as being self-confident and are at ease in the present circumstances. On the other hand, if you observe that a person has a shaky voice or stutters while addressing you, this can probably indicate the fact that they feel uncomfortable or lack confidence in what is being said. In addition, rapid speech may signify anxiousness or panic. Apart from the speech pattern itself, there are other variables that can be drawn from how active an individual is during a conversation. The thing is that some people spend most of their time talking and give the person they have a conversion with little or no time to make their own points. Such people may be overconfident, arrogant, or outright rude. They usually have the belief that what they have to say is much more important than what the other person has to say. Other times, it may be the feelings of insecurity that makes them feel they need to overcompensate.

Interesting enough, some research studies show that people that have a loquacious or extroversive nature appear to be more intelligent than they are. But then the supposed intelligence is going to fade out when they make a remark that looks absurd or does not at all appeal to common sense. People that give room for others to express their view have shown reasonable consideration, and the assumption should not be made that the outward projection that is the exact reflection of their internal processes.

CHAPTER 12

Habitual Behavior

As Warren Buffet said, "the chains of habit are too light to be felt until they are too heavy to be broken." The sum total of a person's habits is probably the best indicator yet of their character. After all, our character profile reflects our average attitude and actions.

The habit a person portrays is the most significant indicator of the kind of character they have. For instance, a naturally helpful person may come across as being generous and selfless from the start if they offer to help you out. That alone can communicate that such a person may be empathetic and genuinely caring.

Someone who prefers to stay indoors almost all day may most likely turn out to be highly introverted. That would definitely not be surprising if you find out they enjoy their own

company much lot than social gatherings.
Someone who literally enjoys hanging out and
socializing may be able to make friends more
easily than someone who does not. Habits dictate
the things we like to do. They facilitate our
hobbies and help us avoid boring chores and
situations. So, being able to discern a person's
habits will give you a huge helping hand in
determining just how they think or act.
Another thing to be put into consideration is the
particular kind of entertainment that the person
enjoys a lot. Some people enjoy sports and
games; others are movie freaks, art lovers, etc.
The kind of entertainment a person gets to enjoy
can set the tone for his character. A lover of the
latest online trends may absolutely love getting
new costumes at any cost. The same goes for all
the entertainment categories. They can
absolutely tell you the hidden truth you want to
know about the person.

The Company They Keep

"Show me your friend, and I will tell you who you are."

This highlights how much of an impact the company and relationships we keep have on us. To analyze someone, your work may be made simpler if you know the traits that their closest friends and associates possess. A lot of our habits are picked up subconsciously from the people closest to use. Their traits rub off us and show up in our own life by default. For instance, if you find yourself in the midst of a tightly knit, outward group of friends, that may likely be because you are outgoing yourself. Even if you are not, though, it could mean that you find that trait about them intriguing enough to want to give it a try.

By way of conclusion, there are several pointers that can help you better profile the stranger standing in front of you. If you are able to pin multiple of these pointers in the same direction with regards to certain traits, then you are on safe

ground. However, you must be careful not to

allow preconceived notions to impede your

judgment.

Chapter 13

Effective Communication

When we are born, we are already well on our way to mastering nonverbal communication. Babies cry, scream, whimper, and coo and the adults who love and care for them respond. The response is the teacher as the child grows and learns which sound to make to get the response they need.

It is this innate survival instinct among all living beings that begins our lifelong lesson in communication. Somewhere along the way however, we humans tend to stop learning how to communicate effectively, believing that if we "use our words" we will get our message delivered in the right way to the right person. Unfortunately, there are many parts to the effective exchange of information and ideas and we would do well to learn more about them.

Communication is not just talking. The word "communication" is derived from an old Latin word "communicare" which means, "to share". When communication is successful both parties understand the information that was shared or divided between the two.

Communication always needs a giver **and** a receiver, and if those two parties involved in the discourse do not reach an understanding (this is different than agreement, although an agreement can be an understanding) then they did NOT communicate, they were just participants in a discourse.

Effective communication consists of several parts: a sender, a receiver, a message, the medium by which the message is delivered (such as spoken word, body language, written word), decoding of message by all parties, feedback, and the "static" or things that interfere with the effective delivery of the message.

The sender is the person who is trying to communicate a message, share information, or persuade another person or persons. The receiver is the person or group for whom the message or information is intended.

The message, an oft overlooked and under considered part of communication is vitally important. I'm sure you have had a conversation with someone at one time or another who didn't seem to have a clue what they were trying to say.

Perhaps they "talked in circles", they raised their voice or spoke too softly, or they overused place holders such as "um", "ah", or "ya know", and to further complicate your understanding, they fidgeted while speaking, paced, wrung their hands, or adjusted their clothing.

When a speaker is certain of what they want to express, what information they want to share, or what emotion they want to convey, their body language will be much more decisive, calmer, more controlled. Their pitch and tone will be even and exude confidence.

Decoding is simply the act of translating what was said by the sender into what it means to the receiver.

Static is the noise or other variables that interfere with the message.

Finally, feedback is quite important to both sender and receiver as it enables the sender to know for certain the information was understood correctly and allows the receiver to express their thoughts about the message.

The three main factors are:

Words we use, or speech, makes up roughly 7% of face to face communication.

Tone, which is the sound of our voice; the inflection, the pace, the enunciation and emphasis of words used, the modulation and pitch. These all give an indication of the sender's thoughts and feelings.

Non-verbal cues, or body language, which includes several factors such as hand use, eye contact, posture, personal space and position, gestures, movements, non verbal sounds such as grunting, snorting, clearing one's throat, and much more.

Of these three, non-verbal communication includes tone and body cues which we will discuss further in the next chapter.

Chapter 14

The Confident Handshake

In the olden times, a handshake was used to show the other person that they are not holding any weapons. Nowadays, the handshake has become a means for greeting or saying goodbye to another person. It is also used for sealing a commercial deal between people of equal status, particularly in Western cultures.

The main reason why people do not initiate handshakes would be due to the uncertainty of the situation. Indeed, there are times when a handshake has to be avoided. Certain cultures (such as those in most Muslim countries) prohibit you from shaking hands with a woman, for instance, because it is considered to be rude.

The best advice when it comes to initiating a handshake is to read the gestures of the other person: if they seem happy to meet you then go ahead. If they seem forced, it is best to greet them by giving out a small nod instead.

How to Give a Confident Handshake

There are generally three types of handshakes:

- Dominant

- Submissive

- Equal

The dominant handshake involves placing your hand over the other person's hand with your palm facing downward. This will compel the other person to have a Palm Up position, which is a sign of submission. The dominant handshake is also very firm, and when overly aggressive can seem to almost be to the point of crushing the other person's hand.

The submissive handshake is the opposite of the dominant one, wherein the palm is facing upward and the hold is limp, often allowing the other person to control the handshake. Sometimes, the person might even limit the handshake to holding the other person's fingers with theirs, instead of grasping the entire palm. This is a kind gesture to offer to elderly who may have pain from a firmer handshake.

To exhibit just the right amount of confidence, you should aim for the handshake that promotes equality. This is done by positioning your palm in a vertical position. Most likely, the other person will mirror the way your hand is held out as well. The pressure of your hold should be based on that of the other person's. If his is weaker than yours, you should also lower your strength. If his is much stronger, kick yours up a notch as well. You will know if you are about to shake hands with a person with a dominant personality if he or she extends it with palms down. To demilitarize this approach, you can reach out by initiating a palm up position first and then putting your left hand over his right to do a "double-handed" handshake.

The double handed handshake will instantly disarm the dominant handshake and make it a more friendly experience for the both of you. Just be careful in choosing the person on which to apply this technique, though as some people may think it is a power struggle and become aggressive.

If you have a tendency to have cold and clammy hands, you might find it helpful to keep a handkerchief in your bag or pocket so that you can quickly wipe your palms right before you meet someone.

Another trick if you do not have a handkerchief is to imagine holding your hands out in front of a warm fireplace to help prevent your hands from breaking out into a cold sweat. This way you can confidently maintain a firm and neutral handshake and give out a smile to ease the

tension.

Chapter 15

Components of Success

Employment, Business, Resources, Information, Growth, Success, Wealth...

Growth

To be successful in life, you have to continuously grow. Growing means continuously feeding your brain with information. Information can come from many resources such as books, videos, audios, and the like. This is why most successful people read more books than anyone else. To get information you need physical materials and people. To get information from material things you will need to be able to manage time, technology, and money. To get information from people you will need to be able to motivate, encourage, and empathize with people.

Information

The is no knowledge that is not power. Information comes in different forms, shapes, and different styles. You need to have the right information for you at that particular point in time. Your brain has different perspectives every second, this is because your brain gathers information literally every second through all your senses therefore the information that you received a second ago will be perceived differently if you get it a second later. This is why you have to continuously learn and grow. This also explains why the is no knowledge that is not power because irrelevant information can be relevant a second later after your perspective has changed.

Management skills

To be able to work with time, technology and money, you will need technical skills such as planning, organizing, designing, and resource control. These four skills are the key management skills. If you have excellent management skills you will be able to use your resources effectively and efficiently to such an extent that you get relevant information that will enable you to achieve success.

Leadership

To be able to motivate, encourage and empathize with people you will need soft skills such as communication, listening, integrity, teamwork, and more. This is also known as leadership skills. If you use your leadership skills effectively you will be able to get all the information that you want and that is relevant for success from people. A leader has to realize that people need to be motivated, they need to be encouraged and they

need to be energized through health and
wellbeing.

Money

Everybody in life needs a source of income. We
need money to survive. We need money to buy
food, shelter, and all the necessary things in life.
Most importantly, we need money to buy
information directly or indirectly. This is why most
people in life get a job or start their own
businesses. Getting a job, making money, and
getting rich will be explained in detail below.

Technology

Technology is one of the biggest physical
materials that can give human beings a huge
competitive advantage to get information. This is
why information technology is changing the world
and this is why the fourth industrial revolution is

in fact information technology. Technology that can get you closer to information is the technology worth keeping.

People

A mind is a very complex organ in a human being. A mind stores all the information that a human being has, and for you to be able to access that information the person has to be in the right emotional state. For a person to be in the right emotional state all their needs will need to be taken care of including health, energy and the need to be motivated.

Principles of success

- Never stop learning.

- Opportunity is always there.

- Thought and action create success.

- Grow, don't compete.

- Guide your thoughts to think positive.

- Save money for opportunities.

- Live below your means.

- Track your expenses daily.

- Be in charge of your own life.

- Don't blame, take responsibility.

- Think big.

- Set SMART goals.

- Accept change.

- Master time management.

- Be around winners.

- Take care of your health.

- Educate yourself.

- Choose your career wisely.

- Invest for every five years.

- Pay off bad debt.

- Avoid lifestyle inflation.

- Marry the right person.

- Don't think about useless things.

- Plan before doing.

- Failure is an opportunity to learn.

- Learn financial literacy.

- Mind your own business.

- Use taxes to your advantage.

Chapter 16

Body Language in Relationship

Find out if he is single

Can you see if he is single?

Is it a stranger you'd like to approach you, it's nice to know if he's busy - and without asking directly. A wedding ring is a disappointing, but clear signal. In addition, it's hard to know who's already in a relationship - especially if the guy is alone or with other men. If he is with a mixed group, there are ways you can check if one of the women present is his girlfriend. It is not quite easy to distinguish between friendship and love, but notice:

Hodan is he touching women?

Especially younger women may find themselves sitting on the lap of a friend so a lady at the lap does not mean they are a couple. Keeping your hand for longer, however, is a clear love mark.

Likewise, you can peel and tie a little to each other in different places, but if a woman's hands dwell on the guy's gull or constantly lie on his upper arm, they probably have something or are on his way to it.

How close are they placed?

Friends can often sit very close, without anything but friendship. But if your eyes are stuck and your legs are wrapped in another woman, or leaning his head off her, you should use your energy elsewhere - so he is already involved.

How does the guy temporarily leave the group? When you are a boyfriend, you would like to give your partner a praise before going to the bathroom and the like. Keep an eye on how he leaves the group and how he does his entrance. Is there anyone just to know that he's gone five minutes - and is there a special woman he "checks in with" again when he comes back?

Step 2 - Control your posture and mimic

Make him clear that you are attractive and interesting

If you want to make a good impression on a man, it's about looking open and welcoming. It's a good idea to put your own posture and mood underneath: You can clean your body language for errors by practicing in front of the mirror. Stand, go and face the mirror and notice if you send the signals you want.

Would you like to approach a person who had organized body and face in those folds? Otherwise, you have to arrange. Your posture is one of the things that tells you the most about you. The way we stand on reflects our past, our personality, and philosophy of life. A rank position equals high self-esteem, and in fact, you can go from signaling bad self-confidence to signal high status just by straightening your back.

Boost your gait by adding extra energy - it seems hugely attractive. Get up, push the pelvis a little and go with long strides, you may wake up! A healthy and confident time has a strong appeal to both sexes. Get the best of your bosom by stretching your shoulders back and running. If you simultaneously push the elbows towards the waist so that the wrist arms protrude, the breasts with a larger waistline appear to be slimmer.

Are you shy and you are having difficulty keeping the guy's eyes long at a time, instead, straighten your eyes to his forehead or nose tip? He will not notice the difference, but for you, the contact is far less intense. When you get safer, you can see him straight in the eyes in short sequences and always return to the "cheating points" if it's overwhelming.

How are you placed in relation to each other

Is he interested? Take the Territory Test

Are you out to eat with someone you want a relationship with, you have good chances to take the temperature if he's ready for you. Mentally, we have to share things and spaces around us into territories, that is, your "page" and "my" page, and we will automatically feel ownership and guard over our own area.

Do you sit and the man on each side of a table, you will each have a part of the table that is "yours". In other words, the table becomes a scene, you can read a lot. Choose a thing on the table, for example. a salt tank. Arrange and move it as randomly as you speak.

When it does not seem too striking, push the thing forward and over on his half of the table. Take your hand while talking on. If he is uninterested, he will feel a bit uncomfortable in fashion over this intrusion into his room and unconsciously find some way to move things back to your part of the table. If he has the thing, he is fine with your approach. If he touches it directly, it is a sign that he is completely wavelength with you and would like to intensify the contact.

Imitate his body language

Blow him up with your body language

Is him you have made yourself insensitive in his body language? In fact, with a little finesse, you may have the luck of wiping a closed guy up if you master the mirror's art by simply imitating his body posture. In general, it is not a good idea to mirror closed or negative body language. But if the guy you want to make an impression on, for example. Standing up a wall with crossed arms, then you start in the same position. That way, you show his subconscious that you share his feelings. Now you speak peacefully about loosely and firmly. Probably, he will start relaxing a little more. Have patience and wait for him to feel comfortable. If his convulsively folded arms become a bit looser, you are well on your way. You can test whether he is opening you by letting your one arm hang loose down the body while the other is still over the chest (elbow grip). Is he with you, he will follow suit. If he holds the closed position, you must also take it again and spend some more time warming him up. Try again to let one arm hang down. Once he has copied, and you still talk together, you can open further by letting both arms hang down the side. Perhaps it takes a long time for him to do the same.

If he cannot loosen up at all, you can arrange him a drink or similar to wipe his arms out of the locked position. When you finally stand breast less against breast without parades between you, do not be able to hurry quickly. Keep calm, do not approach you further or start touching him. Wait for at least 15 minutes if you want to make sure he is thawed up.

Chapter 17

Head Gestures

Where the head goes, the body inevitably follows. Decoding head movements are essential to knowing what a person is thinking. After all, it is where the brain is located.

Generally, when a person is nodding, whether consciously or subconsciously, this means that he agrees to what you are saying. Nodding is not just limited to pronounced upward and downward movements of the head. Be observant of tiny, almost imperceptible nods during a conversation. When a listener is nodding the head slowly and rhythmically, this may mean that he is listening attentively. However, you need to verify this assumption by looking for other non-verbal cues such as the focus of the person's eyes.

When the listener is nodding the head rapidly, this signifies that he has grasped your point and thus, it is time to move on to the next topic. In a way, this head gesture is indicative of impatience. When a person's head is held up, this reveals a neutral state of mind. This means that he is currently receptive to suggestion. So when you see a person's head held up towards you, then that is the perfect time to influence him.

On the other hand, when his head is held up high, this shows firmness and arrogance. Furthermore, when the individual's chin is held up, this reveals pride and defiance. This is especially true if the neck is exposed and extended upward. This is an instinctive response to look taller and bigger and thus, to intimidate the other person.

If a person's head is titled to one side, this exposes vulnerability to suggestion. When the other's head is tilted in such a way that the neck is exposed, this means that he trusts you. When people tilt their heads, it can mean a lot of different things, all depending on the context. It may be used to expressed sympathy or concern. If you were speaking, this means that the person is urging you to continue. In courtship, the head tilted to the side signifies interest. However, when the head is tilted to the side and upwards, it is meant to express a sense of incredulity, as though the person is saying: "Seriously?"

When the individual's head is upright and leaning forward towards you, this shows that he is interested in you or in what you are saying.
On the other hand, of his head is leaning forward in a downward direction, this suggests censure and should warn you of a forthcoming criticism. This is especially true if that person is in a position of authority.
Traditionally, when sideways head shaking is forceful, it is used to show that the person strongly disagrees with you. That said, the shaking of the head from side to side does not

automatically mean disagreement. It may also express an emotion of disbelief. Depending on the context, it may be brought about by frustration.

When head movements are erratic and accompanied by eyes darting about the room, this reveals that the person is experiencing stress of discomfort. It shows him assuming a behavior that is typical of a caged animal.

When a person thrusts the head forward, this gesture springs from the animal instinct to lock on the prey. This shows that he is on aggressive mode. However, when the individual retreats the head, he is on protective mode, much like a turtle going back to the safety of his shell.

Chapter 18

Being conscious of Your Own visual communication

It is not only helpful to be ready to read the body language of the people around you, but it's also important to be ready to read your own body language. this will be a difficult task because it's not always easy to ascertain yourself from a third-party perspective. that's why I recommended that you simply observe yourself during a mirror or maybe through video.

To be ready to read your own body language, you would like to be extremely conscious of your body and therefore the ways during which it moves. you would like to be so aware that you simply can feel the slightest movement, just like the slightest movement of shoulders or legs. You even got to remember of the movements your body doesn't neutralize a selected situation. for instance, you would possibly not be making proper eye contact thus making a conversation a touch awkward. Being conscious of your own body language are often difficult, but it's a particularly important skill to accumulate. during this chapter, we'll check out some things that your body language could also be telling the people around you. By having the ability to urge a handle on your body language, you'll be ready to line up your words together with your actions and movements.

Your body language May Tell

Perhaps the foremost common reason people become curious about reading others through their non-verbal communication is to work out when an individual is lying. The so-called "human lie detectors" aren't gifted individuals who have innate abilities. While they're certainly clever folks, they need simply mastered reading people. For example, they're considerably conversant in eye contact and eye movements. One telltale sign of a lying individual is that the lack of eye contact. However, you'll still devour on lies even when a private makes some extent of not watching you. you'll easily devour on this if your interlocutor has "shifty" eye movements, that is, if they move their eyes from left to right, as if to ascertain if there's anyone coming after them. This eye movement is an involuntary response which will be a sign that something's up.

Your body language May Make Others Feel Good About Themselves

Your body language can even have very positive effects on the folks that you're lecture. If you're touching the person, smiling, laughing, and searching at them quite usual, you'll give them just the boost of self-esteem that they'll be trying to find. Of course, touch are some things you would like to take care with as unsolicited touching can get creepy very quickly.

That being said, facial expressions like smiling, or open gestures like holding your arms out when speaking can go an extended way toward making others feel far more comfortable around you. These sorts of behaviors will signal to your counterpart that you simply are receptive and willing to interact them during a forthcoming manner.

One other important aspect to think about is named "mirroring". once you act during a similar manner as your interlocutor, you appear to be "in synch" with them. What this does is that it creates a pattern during which your counterpart feels comfortable, as if you "get them" at a subconscious level. While we'll be stepping into this into greater detail afterward, it's worth mentioning that you simply can implement this today by simply observing that the opposite person is doing and behaving accordingly.

Your body language May Make Others Upset

If you're doing the other of the items listed above, your subtle actions could have the precise opposite effect. If you retain a distance, don't smile, don't laugh, don't make eye contact, or just don't pay much attention to the person you're talking with, you'll actually make them feel uncomfortable. Also, your tone of voice plays such a crucial role in helping others feel comfortable around you. So, do take the time to form sure that your voice is signaling what you're really feeling at any given time.

Your body language May Confuse Others

Many types of body language are easily understood by the people around us. If we smile at them and stand on the brink of them, they probably feel that we are happy spending time with them and like who they're as an individual. If we ignore the person and ask them without even watching them, they're going to feel the negative tone. If your body language doesn't match up to how you're feeling or if it's very inconsistent, you'll confuse the people around you.

For instance, have you ever encountered a colleague that shakes your hand without watching you? How does that cause you to feel? Does it appear to be this person in tired of you or maybe even dislikes you? If you've got ever been during this situation, you'll appreciate how a scarcity of eye contact can convey a negative message.

Conversely, what if there was a colleague whom you genuinely disliked, but you continue to checked out them and smiled at them often? Would that convey your true feelings? Perhaps you're just being polite so as to spare that person's feelings. Nevertheless, you would possibly be subconsciously sending conflicting messages as other aspects of your body language may divulge your true feelings.

I recall one occasion during which two colleagues who disliked each other greeted one another at a conference. They were both very polite and professional. However, their displeasure for one another become painfully evident as they gave each other a weak handshake despite smiling and exchanging cursory pleasantries. Needless to mention, it got awkward rather quickly.

So, if you would like to avoid having your body language confuse the people around you, you would like to remember of it and confirm that it matches with how you're feeling and the way you are trying to portray yourself.

One other common situation during which your body language can send mixed signals is within the dating world. once you check out smooth-talking individuals who are trying to find love, you regularly see them talking up the proper game, but they completely lack the non-verbal communication to travel with it.

Some smooth talkers have the lines down right, but they don't maintain healthy visual contact, they don't keep a healthy posture and even resort to creepy and cringeworthy touching. In fact, you'll even find that some so-called dating gurus tell their followers to the touch early, and often, in order that the opposite party can get the message that they're interested.

I'll say this again: unsolicited touching are often creepy directly and derail your chances at making a real reference to someone during a matter of seconds.

That is why you would like to concentrate to how you conduct yourself. If you show good posture, smile sort of a normal person would, and respect your interlocut0r's personal space, you'll have an excellent chance at hitting things off without seeming sort of a creepy fella.

Your body language Can cause you to Seem Confident

Body language, facial expressions and gestures generally are often a dead giveaway for confidence of lack thereof. once you are confident, your mannerism will send that message. as an example, confident individuals have square shoulders and appearance straight ahead. While drooping shoulders may simply be bad posture, the very fact of the matter is that your posture will reveal much more than you think that.

In order for your body language to portray confidence, you would like to be keenly conscious of the ways during which you progress and behave. you would like to require powerful body language movements and incorporate them into your day. It are often difficult to vary something that's barely noticeable, but it's certainly a helpful skill to master.

A good rule of thumb to stay in mind is to remember of how your body language lines up

together with your intended message. If you genuinely sort of a person, then confirm that your body language matches your words. Also, if you genuinely dislike an individual, confirm that your body language doesn't offend that individual.
After all, there's nothing wrong with being polite.

Chapter 19

Body Language Cues And Meanings

Body cues and what they signal

We will look at two broad categories when discussing signals and meaning: positive or open body language and negative or closed body language. By reading these cues, you'll figure out how receptive others are to you or the situation. At any given time, a person is either open or closed from their external environment. Whether it's at a BBQ party, a networking event, family gathering, board room meeting, giving a presentation, or dining with you on that first date, people will always show you what state they are in through their non-verbal communication.

Open body language examples

• **Open palms:**

Open palms are a hand gesture that demonstrates openness. Instead of hiding them in their pockets, behind their backs, or holding a closed fist, the person will display their hands. It is usually a sign that the person is being honest and sincere with you.

Evolutionarily, when we see closed palms, our brains receive the signal that we might be in danger (the hidden hands could be carrying a weapon of hiding something life-threatening). Our limbic brain automatically communicates to the rest of the brain, and we become reactive. But sometimes, the other person is simply unaware of their non-verbal communication. So it's not always a good idea to immediately get defensive when you don't see someone's hands. However, it's always a good sign when the person you're talking to is aware enough to show you their open hands.

How you can use it:

When engaged with others in conversation, ensure your hands are open most of the time and that people can see them. It's also best to keep the palms facing upward as much as possible.

The eyebrow flash:

When someone does an eyebrow flash, you'll see their eyebrows raise slightly for a fraction of a second. This is usually a sign of interest. People tend to use this to show professional interest, either to give approval or agree to something. It can also be used to seek confirmation or even thank someone.

Think of it as a quick nonverbal "yes." In a romantic setting, the eyebrow flash indicates romantic interest. It can also be used in a social setting between two friends when they recognize each other. It signals to the other person delight in the encounter. Whenever we use the eyebrow flash, we call attention to the face. Teachers and speakers often use it as a way of saying "Listen to this!" or "Look at me!" depending on context.

Not all cultures see this as a positive cue, however. For example, the Japanese find this cue indecent, so I would avoid it entirely when engaging with Japanese people.

How you can use it:
Use the eyebrow flash when you see someone you like or who you want to like you. Give them a quick eyebrow flash followed by a warm smile. If you're going to get the attention of someone or have them pay closer attention to what you're about to say, raise your eyebrows right before you deliver the message. And if you're on the receiving end of a conversation and want to show

your interlocutor that you're interested, raise your eyebrows!

• The equal handshake:

Have you ever had a really awkward and yucky handshake? Or maybe one that was just downright weak and clumsy? Handshakes are really important when building mutual rapport, and they can tell us a lot about the other person. A handshake can tell us whether the person is nervous, submissive, aggressive, domineering, or confident.

When you shake hands, you want to make sure it's not too firm and dominant, but at the same time, it shouldn't come across as weak. That's why learning an equal handshake is encouraged. There are several elements to a good handshake. Namely, maintaining good eye contact, having a warm, genuine smile, extending your arm with a slight bend at the elbow, keeping your fingers pointed downward while approaching the other person's hand, and most importantly, applying equal pressure during the handclasp. It's also best to lean forward toward the other person and make sure to do a slow release of the handshake after about two seconds. This type of handshake signals mutual respect, openness, confidence, and power. Yet, it leaves the other person feeling warm and fuzzy inside. Whenever you shake someone's hand, and they leave you with that special and good feeling, you can be sure they used this equal handshake technique on you.

How you can use it:

A good rule of thumb is to only shake hands when you know the other person is receptive and open to it. Always think about context and culture before extending a handshake to someone. If they are from Japanese culture, they might prefer a different form of greeting (such as bowing your head). If they are Italian, perhaps a kiss on the cheek is more welcome. If you're unsure how well a handshake will be received, consider a head nod or wait for another person to initiate it.

Always remember the part about applying equal pressure and be mindful of the age group you're interacting with. Older people require less pressure. People of a higher status in society like to determine the length and pressure of the handshake first, so go with that flow and be sure to reciprocate with an equal exchange for maximum bonding.

Mutual gazing

This is another open body signal that shows interest. More prolonged eye contact, especially from people who are of high status, makes us feel favored. That is especially the case when receiving eye contact from celebrities and movie stars. Increased eye contact also indicated the other person might be curious. Please don't confuse with prolonged and direct eye contact, as most people associate that with aggression. Instead, make eye contact when you agree, when you're actively listening and nodding, and when you're exchanging ideas.

Research indicates that making eye contact just 30% of the time significantly increases the likelihood that your interlocutor will remember what you said. Interestingly enough, certain personality types naturally make eye contact while others struggle with this. If you're the type that struggles, start slowly and perhaps make your focal point areas like the forehead or in-between the eyes so the other person can still feel like you're mutually gazing at each other.

How you can use it:

Do a bit more eye gazing when you wish to bond with someone. Don't make it too direct and unnatural, as you might come across the wrong way. Make sure to glance away occasionally and only look them in the eyes with a soft face when the context of the conversation permits it.

The head tilt

The head tilt is when a person tilts to one side, exposing their neck. This indicates openness because the neck is one of the most vulnerable areas in a person's body. The skin on the neck is much thinner and requires more protection, so when someone exposes their neck and throat, they are essentially opening up. They are showing you that they are comfortable enough around you to be vulnerable.

You'll often see a head tilt from women, especially if they are attracted to you. Still, it can also be used to indicate platonic interest. When a man does it, they usually indicate curiosity about what you're saying, especially if the head tilt is combined with a head nod. Studies of paintings in the last two millennia show that women are depicted three times often as men using the head tilt. Even in modern advertisements, we tend to see a woman tilting her head more often than we see men.

How you can use it:

See it more as a disarming behavior and use it whenever you want to ease a tense situation or get someone to open up. But don't use it too much, especially in official meetings or during sales pitches when the last thing you want is to come off "soft" and exposed.

Closed body language examples

Crossed arms

Crossed arms are one of the most common cues for closed body language that you'll encounter. Practically everyone crosses their arms at some point or another. Most people do this are a protective or coping mechanism. They are likely to cross their arms when projecting anger, anxiety, stress, or even trying to soothe themselves from these emotions. Crossed arms are often done in public. I challenge you to observe yourself to see if you ever cross your arms while alone in the comfort of your home.

Sometimes you might notice someone will clench their fist and combine that with the crossing of the arms, tightening of the lips, or clenching their teeth. Research of over 1500 volunteers was conducted to find out exactly how the crossed-arms gesture made people feel. The volunteers were divided into two groups while attending a series of lectures. The first group was asked to keep their legs uncrossed, arms folded, and to take a relaxed sitting position. The second group did the same, except they were asked to cross their arms throughout the lectures. The outcome was that the second group learned and retained 38% less information than the group with unfolded arms. They were also more critical in their opinions about the lecturers and the lectures.

Of course, you need to be aware of other cluster cues to help you determine whether one is feeling cold or simply closing you off. And if you'd like to know how to handle someone with crossed arms, keep reading because later in the book, we'll talk about different ways to handle difficult people and their personalities.

Crossed legs

This is when the feet are crossed, and one ankle lies on top of the other. It can be done while sitting, standing, or with feet on the table/stool. A person crossing their ankles typically indicates that they are uncomfortable and closed off. The tighter their ankles are locked in, the anxiety or stress the person might be experiencing. But there are some exceptions to this rule. For example, women wearing dresses or skirts tend to sit with their ankles locked which is generally not associated with a closed body language. However, if done for a prolonged period, it might be negative non-verbal communication. Another exception to this is when you see ankles crossed while legs are outstretched on the floor. This can be a relaxed posture with the legs taking up space.

An extreme example of crossed legs is when a person locks their feet around the legs of a chair.

That usually occurs under high-stress situations. I call this the "ejection seat" position because you'd only expect one to have such a position if they were about to be launched out of their seat.

Neck rubbing

When people rub their necks, they usually mask their feelings of insecurity or mounting stress. For others, it's a stress-relieving mechanism. According to scientific studies, when the vagus nerve (the nerve on the side of the neck) is massaged, acetylcholine, a neurotransmitter that sends signals to the heart, causes the heart rate to go down. In more extreme cases, you might see the suprasternal notch (the part where your neck meets your clavicle) being touched. According to various studies, those who habitually rub the neck tend to be more pessimistic or critical than others.

Hand gestures

A hand gesture is part of body language communication. One moves their hands to accentuate or communicate an idea. Gestures influence the meaning we derive from a given message. When a person makes distinct hand gestures, they tend to come across as more confident.

If you're making hand gestures, I recommend keeping your hands between the top of your chest to the bottom of your waist. Moving your hands too high or too low can be distracting to your interlocutor. Now let's look at some common hand gestures and what data they can give you to analyze someone.

• Thumbs up: In many parts of the world, the thumbs-up is generally recognized as a sign of agreement. But if you are visiting Bangladesh, please avoid using this at all costs as it is considered an extreme insult.

• Thumbs down: Thumbs down is generally accepted as a "bad" or "no good" gesture. But did you know that during Roman times, this gesture was used to spell out death? Thank goodness there were no emojis at that time. Imagine how much trouble you'd be in if a Roman soldier sent you an emoji thumbs-down! As a general rule, even today (though we are no longer in the era of the Gladiator), someone sending you a thumbs-down gesture probably doesn't agree with your words, actions, or mannerisms. It can be viewed as a bit childish for someone to physically use this. Still, if you're having a virtual meeting or exchanging a chat, it's pretty standard for adults to use this gesture. It just means you need to establish a more positive rapport because your

interlocutor is not amused by the current
conversation.

Body movements

How we hold our bodies can relay critical data for
a keen observer. For instance, now that you know
about open and closed body language, realize
that when you see someone sitting with a closed
posture, they could be hostile, unfriendly, and
anxious. By contrast, someone with an open
posture may indicate that they are open, friendly,
and willing to interact with you. Posture can tell
us a lot about a person's personality, how
confident they are and whether or not they want
to engage in conversation with us.
If your interlocutor is sitting up straight, they
convey that they are focused and present to
what's going on. Sitting with the body hunched
forward could imply that the person is indifferent,
bored, or distracted by something. While reading

body language, try to notice some of the signals the person is sending.

Decoding the mouth:

Although you might think smiling is always a good thing, different smiles mean different things. The way a person smiles and how they position the lips tells you a lot.

With a truly genuine smile, the corners of the mouth turn upward, and the eyes narrow and wrinkle at the corners. Insincere smiles generally won't involve the eyes. Most of the time, a person will smile insincerely when they are hiding discomfort. You might also notice a partial smile or a smirk which often accompanies displeasure or contempt. This usually suggests disdain, dislike, or uncertainty. If the person you're talking to smiles and combines that with lasting eye contact, a long glance, or a head tilt, that could be an indication of attraction or romantic interest.

When it comes to the lips, compressed or narrowed lips could be indicative of unease. Quivering lips tend to suggest emotions of fear or sadness. Pursed lips are often signaling disagreement or brewing anger. When a person has open, slightly parted lips, it generally means they feel at ease and very relaxed around you.

What the eyes can tell you:

The eyes are often called the windows of the soul. By observing someone's eyes, you can deduce their mood, level of interest, and the hidden emotions they don't want you to know.

Blinking: If a person blinks rapidly, they are usually under some form of stress. Most people assume rapid blinking suggests dishonesty, but that isn't factual. Sometimes people blink when they're uncomfortable, afraid, worried about something, or working through a difficult problem.

Pupil dilation: Pupils dilate when we feel positively toward something or someone. Dilation happens in response to the arousal of the nervous system. Sometimes you'll see someone's pupil dilating either because there's a romantic attraction taking place or because they are infuriated or greatly afraid. If a person is bored and displeased, the pupils usually contract and get smaller.

Gaze direction: If you're trying to have a read of what someone is really interested in, just track the movement of their gaze. Our eyes can't help but wonder and follow what most interests us in any given situation. So if you're sitting across someone and you notice their gaze keeps moving in the direction of the buffet table, perhaps it's a good idea to save the talk until after they've eaten because nothing you say will be of greater value than their desire to eat at that moment. If you're having dinner with a woman and she keeps staring at the door or outside, then it's likely she would rather leave as soon as possible. You need to figure out whether it's you she doesn't want to be around or the restaurant.

People also move their eyes around when recalling information or memories while working through a problem or thinking about something difficult. Interestingly, the eyes tend to move downward or to one particular side depending on a person's personality and baseline. Yet another important reason to identify baselines first and foremost.

Engage in conversation with someone who keeps covering their eyes with their hands, rubbing their eyes, squinting, or closing their eyes briefly (long unnatural blinks). It could be that the person is feeling distressed or irritated, but they don't want to tell you. Some people block their eyes when faced with something they don't particularly want to deal with. Still, it could also be a show of disagreement or reluctance. For instance, your colleague knows it's their turn to work overtime on the weekend, but they want to clock out before you. When you call them out, instead of arguing, they unconsciously raise their hands to their eyes and then quietly and stressfully drag their feet back to their desk.